COWBOYS

LIGHTER

"THE RACE OF RACES"

COWBOYS

A LIBRARY OF CONGRESS BOOK

BY MARTIN W. SANDLER

Introduction by James H. Billington, Librarian of Congress

HarperCollins*Publishers*

For Christopher, Winslow, Robbie and Sarah.
Like children everywhere, with their laughter and their special wisdom they teach us all we know of magic.

ACKNOWLEDGMENTS
The author wishes to thank Robert Dierker, former senior advisor for multimedia activities of the Library of Congress, and Dana Pratt, former director of publishing of the Library of Congress, for their important contributions to this book. Appreciation is expressed to Kate Murphy, Carol Weiss, Heather Henson, the staff of the Prints and Photographs Division of the Library of Congress and Dennis Magnu of the Library's Photoduplication Service. Thanks are due also to Judith Gray, Gerald Parsons and Joseph Hickerson of the American Folklife Center at the Library of Congress.
Once again, a very special note of appreciation is expressed to Kate Morgan Jackson, whose skill and guidance in shaping and editing this book shines through on every page.

◆

Cowboys
A Library of Congress Book
Copyright © 1994 by Eagle Productions, Inc.

Library of Congress Cataloging-in-Publication Data
Sandler, Martin W.
Cowboys ; a Library of Congress book / by Martin W. Sandler ; introduction by James H. Billington.
p.   cm.
ISBN 0-06-023318-4. — ISBN 0-06-023319-2 (lib. bdg.) — ISBN 0-06-446745-7 (pbk.)
Summary: Presents, in text and illustrations, an overview of the life and legend of the American cowboy.
1. Cowboys—West (U.S.)—Juvenile literature.   2. West (U.S.)—Social life and customs—Juvenile literature.   [1. Cowboys—West (U.S.)   2. West (U.S.)—Social life and customs.]   I. Title.
F596.S17   1994
978—dc20
93-2

Design by Tom Starace with Jennifer Goldman
❖
Visit us on the World Wide Web!
http://www.harperchildrens.com

Our type of democracy has depended upon and grown with knowledge gained through books and all the other various records of human memory and imagination. By their very nature, these records foster freedom and dignity. Historically they have been the companions of a responsible, democratic citizenry. They provide keys to the dynamism of our past and perhaps to our national competitiveness in the future. They link the record of yesterday with the possibilities of tomorrow.

One of our main purposes at the Library of Congress is to make the riches of the Library even more available to even wider circles of our multiethnic society. Thus we are proud to lend our name and resources to this series of children's books. We share Martin W. Sandler's goal of enriching our greatest natural resource—the minds and imaginations of our young people.

The scope and variety of Library of Congress print and visual materials contained in these books demonstrate that libraries are the starting places for the adventure of learning that can go on whatever one's vocation and location in life. They demonstrate that reading is an adventure like the one that is discovery itself. Being an American is not a patent of privilege but an invitation to adventure. We must go on discovering America.

James H. Billington
The Librarian of Congress

No figure in this nation's past has been more celebrated or imitated than the American cowboy, who became a legend even as he rode the range. Though his time on the American scene was relatively short, he became an even bigger legend almost as soon as he passed into history.

The cowboy's saga is filled with more than its share of myths and tall tales. Yet his true story is even more remarkable than the fiction that surrounds him. Raw courage, a deep respect for nature and a fierce spirit of independence—these are the qualities that mark the cowboy. Who he really was and what he really did provide us with one of America's greatest adventure stories.

MARTIN W. SANDLER

AN AMERICAN HERO

He is perhaps the greatest of all our heroes. More songs have been written about him and more movies have been made about him than about any other figure in American history.

ince he first came on the scene, magazines and books have been filled with stories about him. Some of the stories are true. Many are not, but they add to the myths that surround him.

H e is the American cowboy, and he needs no invented myths to celebrate him.

The real story is heroic enough. It is a story of men and women on horseback who turned hard work, open spaces and brave deeds into a much-envied way of life.

A COWBOY'S LIFE

The cowboy has a tough job to do. He is in the saddle ten to fourteen hours a day. Much of his time is spent on the range tending the cattle, chasing stray steers and calves and mending fences. Each spring he is involved in rounding up the cattle, branding the calves and then leading the herds over long trails to distant markets. Most of the cowpunchers are young—in their twenties. Many are teenagers.

Everything a cowboy wears has a purpose. His wide-brimmed hat shields him from the sun and the rain. The chaps he wears over his trousers protect him from the prickly underbrush through which he rides. His high-heeled boots keep his feet from pushing through the saddle's stirrups. On the ground, his boots allow him to get a firm footing while he brings a roped steer to a halt.

The cowhand is at the center of the giant American cattle industry. Between the late 1860's and the late 1890's, the cattle he raises will supply much of the meat that will help feed a rapidly growing nation. In that brief time, more than 40,000 cowboys will raise over nine million cattle and herd them overland to far-off railroad centers. There they will be shipped to even more distant slaughterhouses and meat-packing plants.

The cowboy is a special [kind] of person. He is in love [with] nature, particularly with [the] great open spaces of the Amer[ican] West. He has a deep res[pect] and caring for the animals aro[und] him. Above all, he places pers[onal] freedom before everything [else.] His way of life becomes the e[nvy] of millions of his fellow Am[eri]cans, who live in crowded c[ities] and work in stifling factories.

I never hankered for to plow or hoe,
And punching steers is all I know.
With my knees in the saddle and
*   a-hanging to the sky,*
Herding dogies up in heaven in the sweet
*   by-and-by.*

—From song, "The Old Chisholm Trail"

owboys spend most of their time on horseback, and they need to change to a fresh horse three or four times a day. Ranch owners supply the animals, but they are wild and need to be broken in. It takes several weeks and many bone-jarring sessions to tame a bucking bronco, a task that tests the courage and skill of every cowboy who attempts it.

Breaking horses is a dangerous job. On the large ranches, called broncobusters are hired to break in the wild ho But even these specially trained cowboys often meet disaster. Over the years, far more cowpunchers will be ously injured or even killed in accidents on horseback than ir more romantic gunfights that will later fill movie and televi screens.

Any cowboy who says he ain't never been throwed is a liar.

—Cowboy saying

ver the years, many myths will grow up around the American cowboy. In truth, most cowboys will never see a Native American, let alone fight one. Very few will have the chance to rescue beautiful women. But one fact will not be exaggerated: The cowboys will spend their s in the saddle, and their fame as horsemen will be well deserved.

ost of the horses that the cowboys ride are descendants of animals brought to America by the Spanish. In fact, almost everything cowboys wear or use is borrowed from Spanish-speaking cattlemen called *vaqueros* who, the late 1700's, brought their horses, cattle and skills from xico into Texas. It is the *vaquero* who is the true ancestor of American cowboy.

The cowboys come from many different backgrounds. Some are veterans of the Civil War. Many are young men from the East looking for adventure, and almost all are seeking a new way of life. Many of them are African Americans. At the height of the cattle trade, more than 5,000 African-American cowboys will work on ranches, large and small, throughout the West.

Many of the African-American cowboys are ex-slaves from Texas. During their days in slavery they broke horses and herded cattle. They are excellent horsemen. Some work the ranch for a while and then find a new occupation. They become members of all-black units in the United States cavalry, where they carry out a proud record.

any African-Ameri-
can cowboys are
freemen from the
North. Several of
cowpunchers will
me famous for their
g, roping and bronco-
ing skills. The most
us of all will be Bill
ett, who develops a
d-new method of throw-
nd holding a steer by
g into its lower lip as a
log might do. Thanks
m, the term "bulldog-
" becomes an impor-
part of the cowboys'
uage.

Not all the cowpunchers are men or boys; some are women. Throughout the West there are cowgirls who work the range and take part in cattle drives. Many are the wives and daughters of ranch owners. A few own their own ranches.

Cowgirls live in a man's world. have to prove themselves every Those who are successful lear ride, rope and shoot as well as male counterparts do.

PAWNEE BILL'S HISTORIC WILD WEST

AMERICA'S NATIONAL ENTERTAINMENT

BEAUTIFUL DARING WESTERN GIRLS AND MEXICAN SEÑORITAS IN A CONTEST OF EQUINE SKILL.

SEÑORITA ROSALIA

In fact, some cowgirls become even more skilled than most of the men. Before their days on the range are over, many cowgirls will be hired to show off their talents in the wild west shows that will become so popular around the world. One of the great stars of several of these shows will be Annie Oakley, who demonstrates that she can outshoot almost any man in the West. Audiences everywhere applaud the skill and daring of these hard-shooting, hard-riding women.

Last night as I lay on the prairie
And looked at the stars in the sky,
I wondered if ever a Cowgirl
Could get to that "Sweet By-and-By."

—From song, "The Cowgirl's Dream"

THE OPEN RANGE

The wild west shows, the movies, and later television programs will glamorize what the cowboy does. But in reality what he does most is work, and most of his work is done on the range. The vast prairie of the American West, covered with free public grass upon which cattle graze, is what makes the giant cattle industry possible. This industry is so large that by the middle of the 1880's, the cattle-range area of the United States covers almost 1,400,000 square miles, or 44 percent of the entire nation.

illions of cattle roam the range, and it's up to the cowboy to look after them. Some cowmen work for small family ranches. Others work on ranches so large they cover more than two hundred square miles. His work on the range can keep the cowpuncher away from the ranch for days at a time. Often his horse and the cows he tends are his only companions.

It's a tough job. The weather on the prairie can be fierce. Summers are f with scorching heat, wild lightning dust storms. Winter brings bitter cold blizzards that cover the land with moun of snow. It's hard on the cattle, and harder on the men who tend them.

The good thing about talkin' to your horse is he don't talk back.

—Cowboy saying

ending cattle is a dangerous job. Steers often wander away from the grazing herd. They themselves caught between sharp rocks or sometimes stray toward the edges cliffs, and it's the cowboys' to rescue them.

The greatest danger comes from a stampede. The cattle are easily spooked. Any unexpected noise or flash of light, like thunder and lightning, can send thousands of animals charging off in panic. Hundreds of cowboys are killed or injured trying to bring terrified herds back under control.

Tending the range is a never-ending job. While the main band of cowboys keeps watch over the herd, other cowhands ride along the fences that mark the borders of the ranch. The fences, which stretch for miles, must continually be checked and repaired. Especially during the bitter cold winter months, fence riding is the loneliest task of all.

I'm a poor lonesome cowboy,
I'm a poor lonesome cowboy,
I'm a poor lonesome cowboy,
And a long way from home.

—From song, "Poor Lonesome Cowboy"

ork on the range continues through the night. Cowhands take turns making sure that the herd is calm and that there are no cattle thieves about. Only when his night watch is over can the cowboy have his last smoke of the day and get ready for bed.

Despite the hard work and the dangers, the cowboy would never trade his job for life in the city or work in a factory or store. He has little free time, but when he does, he spends it staging horse races or playing cards with companions who share his love of a rough-and-tumble, independent way of life.

When a cowboy's lonesome,
  when a cowboy's blue,
When he's having trouble,
  there's just one thing to do,
Saddle up his pony any kind o' day,
Take out o'er the prairie,
  and ride his cares away.

—From song, "Ride Cowboy"

There are no stores or shops on the ranch, the range or the trail. Most cowboys get to town only once or twice a year. They depend on themselves and each other for safety on the job and for simple everything like a shave or a haircut.

Most of all it is his love of life in the out-of-doors that marks the American cowboy. Artists of the day portray him as a man surrounded by open spaces and sky. Their pictures reveal him also as a man far removed from civilization, home and loved ones.

ROUNDUP!

Each part of the year brings special duties and special events. The first of these is the spring roundup. During the roundup the cattle are brought together and counted, newborn calves are branded, and four- and five-year-old cows are selected to be driven to market.

The type of saddle most cowboys use is one first introduced by the *vaqueros*. Made of leather and set on a wooden frame, it is the cowhand's most valuable piece of equipment. Some are fancier than others, but all of them have a horn at the front. During roundups the horn is used as a hitching post for the rope with which the cowhand lassoes cattle.

The spring roundup usually begins in May and lasts between thirty and forty days. Cowboys from various ranches within a district join together to round up the cows. It's a difficult job requiring special skills on the part of both the cattlemen and the horses they ride.

Once a band of c[attle] has been gath[ered] together, the [cow]boys must sep[arate] the calves to be bra[nded] from the older c[attle] which will be taken [up] the trail to far-off rail[road] centers. This "cu[tting] out" process requires [the] greatest of skills. C[ow] hands ride horses [spe]cially trained to stop [and] turn sharply wit[hout] spooking the rest o[f the] herd into a stampede[.]

A cow outfit is no better than its horses.

—Cowboy saying

nce a cow or calf is separated from the herd, the cowboy then has to toss his rope over the animal's head and bring it to a halt. His horse must carry him at just the right speed to keep up with the cow, and then must stop and dig its hooves into the earth once the cow has been roped.

N ow comes the most dangerous job of all. One or two cowhands toss another rope around the hind legs of the halted calf and throw the animal to the ground. It's a process accompanied by swirling dust and sharp, flying hooves. It's a rare cowboy who repeats this task throughout the roundup without suffering some kind of injury.

nce the calf is hog-tied on the ground, it is ready for branding. On some ranches the animal is dragged into a specially built branding corral. On others the branding is done on the spot where the animal is grounded.

It's the man that's the cowboy, not the outfit he wears.

—Cowboy saying

randing is done with a red-hot iron in the shape of the special mark of the ranch that owns the animal. This custom is also borrowed from the *vaqueros*. Some people criticize the system, saying that it is cruel to the animals. But the ranch owners reply that it is the only way to prove that particular cattle belong to them. They also point out that it is the only way to discourage the gangs of cattle thieves who roam the West.

The Lazy J Brand

The Scissors Brand

The Quarter Circle T Brand

The Flying V of the Matador Ranch

The Four Sixes Brand

The Seven Up Brand

The Rocking Chair Brand

here are as many diffe branding marks as there ranches and ranch own Some are simple; others more elaborate. Some cows cha hands so many times and branded so often that they begi look like walking billboards.

During the roundup the cowboys are served their meals by a cook, who operates out of what is called the chuckwagon. The wagon has a hinged board on the back t folds down to make a worktable. Inside are partments and drawers that hold tin plates cups, knives, forks and spoons, and such ba- items in the cowboy's diet as coffee, sugar, d or canned fruit, rice, beans and flour. Basic dicines are also stored in the chuck wagon, g with various horse liniments.

Food, Plates, Cups, etc.

Tool Box

Rear View

Cover

Bows

Driver's Seat

Bedroll

Water Barrel

Chuck Box

Wagon Bed

Boot

Brake

Iron Tire

Side View

The roundup is more than a working event. It is one of the few times that cowhands from various ranches work in the same area, and it gives them the chance to eat together and to swap stories and experiences. Most roundups end with a giant dance and barbecue, which becomes the main social event in the cowboys' year.

There were usually about fifteen chuck wagons and more than 400 cowhands from ranches all over the county. We sang, we bragged, we laughed. We all looked forward to it.

—Unpublished diary of a cowboy, 1879

Whenever cowhands get together, they are sure to exchange stories. The cowboys are great storytellers. Many of the myths that grow up around them come from the tall tales they tell about themselves and their companions around the nightly campfire. These stories will become an important part of American folklore.

ON THE TRAIL DRIVE

Many cowpunchers' stories are about their experiences driving cattle to market. The trail drive is the longest and most challenging part of the cowboys' lives. It involves two or three thousand head of cattle, more than fifty horses and ten to twelve cowhands. The trail drive, says one cowboy, is "an endless grind of worry and anxiety which only a strong physical frame could stand."

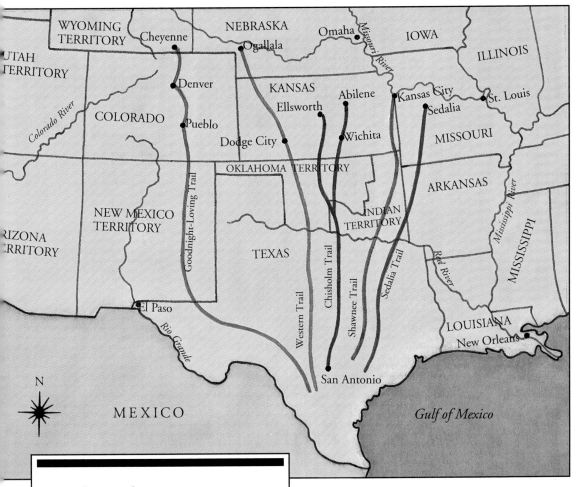

There are several main routes the cattlemen can follow as they drive the thundering herds northward to the railroad yards. The Western Trail begins in Texas and extends all the way into the Dakota Territory. The Shawnee Trail leads to Missouri railroad centers in Kansas City, Sedalia and St. Louis. The Goodnight Loving Trail leads through New Mexico, Colorado and Wyoming. The most popular of all routes is the Chisholm Trail. It leads to the Kansas towns of Dodge City and Abilene, which become the busiest of all the railroad centers.

Early in the spring we round up the dogies, Mark 'em and brand 'em and bob off their tails; Drive up our horses, load up the chuck wagon, Then throw the dogies out on the trail.

—From song, "Git Along, Little Dogies"

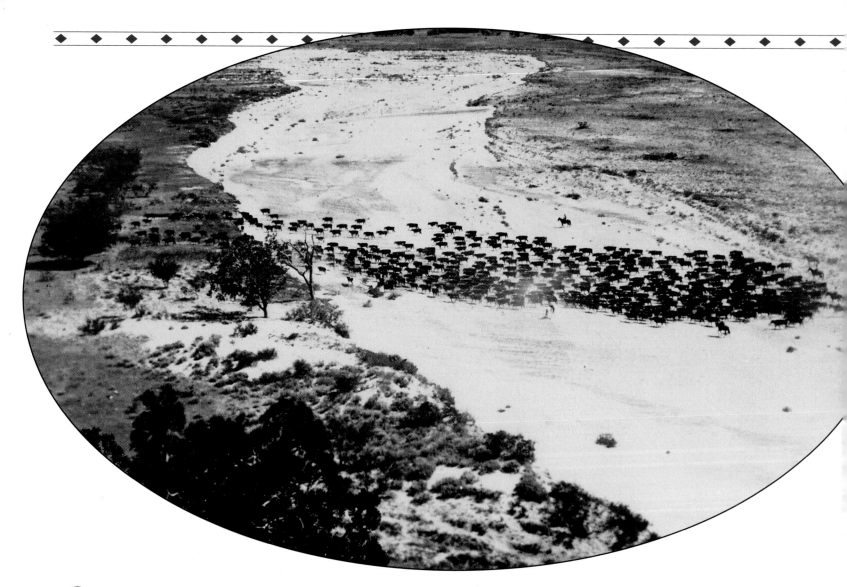

On the trail, each cowboy has his own special task and position. The herd is driven in a long straight with a veteran cowhand on each side at the front "point" positions. These cowhands set the pace the cattle and lead them in the right direction. On each side "flank" position of the herd ride pair cowpunchers who make sure that the cattle stay within the herd. At the rear "drag" position, catch the continual dust kicked up by the cattle, ride the youngest and least experienced of the cowpokes. F start to finish the drive is headed by a trail boss. Along with making sure each cowboy does his job, the boss decides how far the outfit will travel each day and where it will stop and bed down for the night.

The chuck wagon, so important to the cowboys during roundup, is even more vital during the long days and nights of the trail drive. Carrying the outfit's food, equipment and medical supplies, it travels alongside the trail and slightly ahead of the herd. Pulled by two or four mules, the wagon is driven by the cook, who is hired more for his driving ability than for his skill at preparing meals.

The cook is usually older than the cowhands and is often a former cowboy himself. Besides driving the chuck wagon, he sets up camp every night, fixes the meals and serves as nurse and doctor to the men and animals. The cowboys love to play pranks and jokes on the cook, but they all know how important he is to the success of the drive.

The best seasoning for range cooking is a salty sense of humor.

—Cowboy saying

During the first few days of the trail drive, the cowhands push the cattle along at a rapid pace of more than twenty miles a day. This gets the animals used to being driven and keeps them from turning and running back to the range they know as home. Once the routine has been established, the pace is slowed to about fifteen miles a day. Over time, too quick a pace will take weight off the cattle, and the heavier they are when they get to market, the greater the price they will bring.

Most of the cattle that the cowboys drive over trail are Texas longhorns. They are nervous mals, quick to stampede. They can be feroc as well. But they are extremely hardy. They survive on small amounts of grass and can go up to days without water. Most important for the drive, longhorns can travel for miles without getting tired

The cowboy's life on the drive is filled with danger. He can be thrown from his mount while feeling his way over rocks into which cattle have strayed. He can be kicked by a horse, charged by a steer or trampled in a stampede. There is no turning back if he breaks a bone or becomes sick on the trail miles from his home ranch.

The bones of men and animals that lie bleaching along the trails abundantly testify that this was not the first instance in which the plain had baffled man.

——From *Log of a Cowboy*, Andy Adams

The crude graves of cowpunchers who die on the trail serve as grim reminders of the price many men and boys pay for choosing the life of a cowhand. There are many cowboy tales of those whose journeys end in places not found on any map.

Much of the long cattle trail runs through empty, forbidding territory. Many parts of these unse[ ] areas are breathtakingly beautiful. Some are framed by majestic mountains. Others contain [ ] flowing rivers. But the rivers present some of the greatest hazards of all. Frightened cattle and h[ ] have to be driven across them. Many rivers, calm and shallow during most of the year, become [ ] and treacherous after heavy spring rains. Men and animals face the danger of drowning every time the[ ] counter a river.

Oh, some boys go up the
　　trail for pleasure,
But that's where they gets it
　　most awfully wrong;
For you have no idea the
　　trouble they give us,
While we go a-driving
　　them along.

—From song, "Git Along, Little Dogies"

The long cattle dri[ve] [is] as hard on the h[orses] as it is on the [cow-] hands. Each co[wboy] must change his mou[nt at] least three times a day[. He] gets his fresh horses [from] the large herd of ani[mals] that are driven beside [the] chuck wagon ahead o[f the] cattle. The horse her[d is] called the *remuda*, a Sp[anish] word meaning "rep[lace-] ment." Each morning [each] cowboy enters the *re[muda]* and selects his first m[ount] of the day.

T he cowhand who looks after the *remuda* is called a wrangler. He is most often the least experienced member of the trail outfit, a youngster learning to be a cow- boy. The wrangler sees to it that the replacement horses are well fed. He rounds them up whenever the cowboys are ready to change their mounts.

s night falls on the trail, the cowboys gather near the chuck
wagon to swap stories and songs. Their long day is still not
over. During the night each will have to take his turn
patrolling the herd. But for most cowhands, the time at the
ing campfire is filled with the most treasured moments of all.
y have worked hard. They have even risked their lives. Now, in
quiet beauty of a vast, uninhabited land, they find time to relax
others who best understand why they have been drawn to a life
ifferent from that of most Americans.

*[The cowboys are] as hardy
and self-reliant as any men
who ever breathed—with
bronzed, set faces, and keen
eyes that look all the world in
the face without flinching as
they flash out from under
their broad-brimmed hats.*

—Theodore Roosevelt,
The Winning of the West

or all the cowboys there are t[imes]
when it seems that their days [and]
nights on the trail will never [end.]
But on every drive there co[mes]
the moment when someone at the h[ead]
of the herd shouts out that he has s[pot]-
ted, rising out of the wide prairie, [the]
far-off cattle town to which they [have]
been headed for so long. Exc[ited]
cowhands pick up the pace and d[rive]
the cattle into the town.

heir work is still not over. The cattle, which have
picked up the cowboys' excitement, must be calmed
down and led into wooden pens, where they will be
sold to the highest bidder.

Finally the cattle are sold, loaded onto railroad cars and made ready for their final journey to the slaughterhouses. For the first time in months, the cowboys can truly relax.

ON THE TOWN

While they are on the drive, the cowboys have little or no money in their pockets. Even if they have some, there is no place to spend it on the trail. As soon as the drive is over, the trail boss gives them their pay. Whooping and hollering, the cowpunchers head for the delights of town.

en we reached Dodge
City, we drew our four
months' pay.
...es was better then, boys,
than they are today.
...way we drank and
...ambled and [danced]
...he girls around—
... a crowd of Texas cow-
...boys has come to take our
...own.

rom song, "John Garner's Trail
Herd"

The towns are filled with saloons, dance halls, gamblers and liquor. Months of hard, lonesome work is forgotten as the cowboys let off steam.

BITTERS

On the trail, the cowboys have worn the same clothes for weeks, bathed in cold streams, slept on the hard ground and eaten the same monotonous meals repeatedly. In town they eat at real tables, bathe in rooming-house bathtubs and indulge themselves with new clothes. After weeks of tedious routine in each other's company, they look for entertainment and female companionship.

The most popular places are the many saloons that fill every frontier town. Here the cowboys line up at the bar and find out what has been happening during the long weeks they have been on the trail and out of touch with the world.

There are less cutthroats and murderers graduated from the cowboy than from the better class who come from the east for venture of gain.

—Mayor of Dodge City, c. 1880

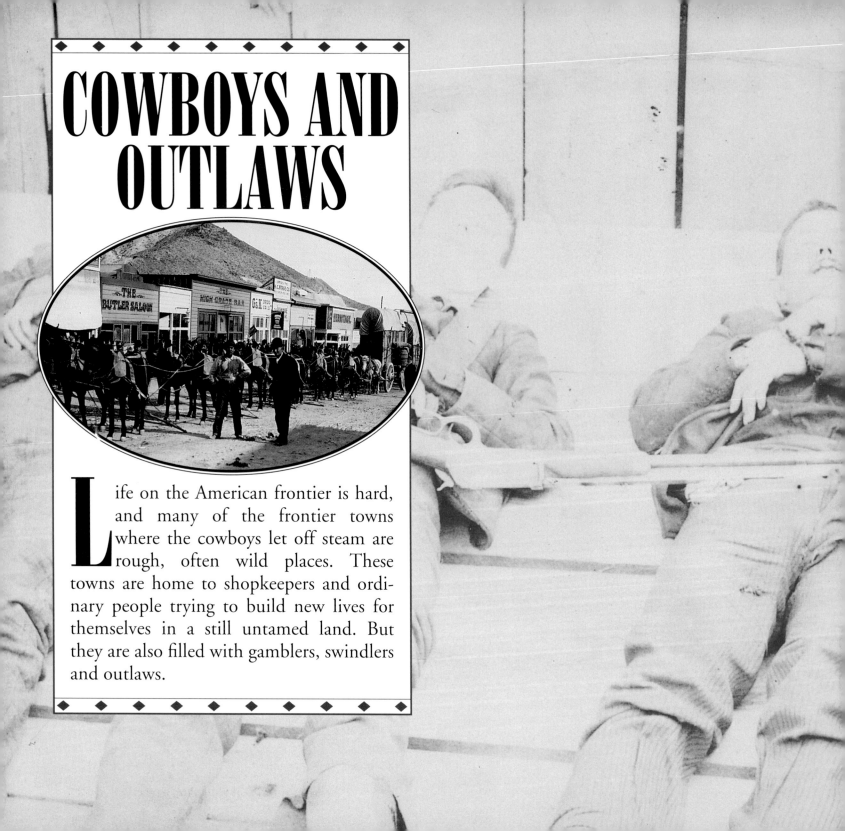

COWBOYS AND OUTLAWS

Life on the American frontier is hard, and many of the frontier towns where the cowboys let off steam are rough, often wild places. These towns are home to shopkeepers and ordinary people trying to build new lives for themselves in a still untamed land. But they are also filled with gamblers, swindlers and outlaws.

THE GREAT TRAIN ROBBERY

...ax of this 1896 play, a car rolled on stage, dynamite was lit and the sides of the car shattered. One playgoer, the inventor Thomas

...NSATIONAL AND STARTLING "HOLD UP" OF THE GOLD EXPRESS, BY FAMOUS WESTERN OUTLAWS.

Edison, was so impressed that he turned the drama into a motion picture, which, as the first Western, became one of the most famous movies eve...

The untamed West attracts people who operate with no regard for the law. They rob banks, hold up trains, steal cattle and horses and terrorize people who have come to the West seeking new opportunities.

The place is fast becoming civilized, several men having been killed there already.

—*Deseret* (Utah) *News,* 1869

Most cowboys do not come face-to-face with the outlaws. Once the cowboys have spent their time town after the trail drive, they make their way back to the ranch, where the cycle of raising the cat rounding them up and driving them to market is repeated. But the West is filled with cattle thie who try to rob ranch owners of their animals, so cowboys do occasionally have bloody encoun with cattle thieves.

n places where there is little organized law enforcement, private citizens often take the law into their own hands. Posses are formed to hunt down the bandits. Groups called vigilantes hold hastily called trials and pass sentence on laws who are caught.

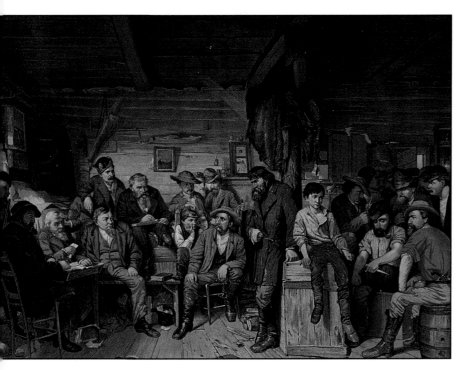

he sentences that are passed down and carried out by the vigilantes are harsh. For accused murderers, bank robbers and horse thieves alike, frontier justice often means death at the end of a rope.

The gun and the rope become symbols of Western law and order. Private companies such as Wells Fargo, an express agency that transports gold and silver from western mine fields, hire armed guards to accompany all their shipments.

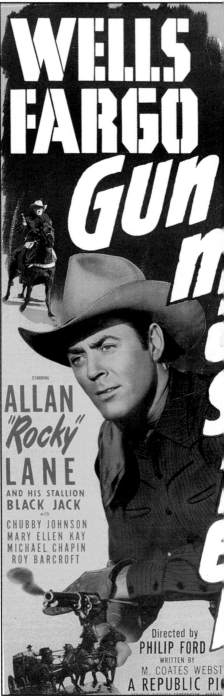

WELLS FARGO Gun master

STARRING

ALLAN "Rocky" LANE
AND HIS STALLION BLACK JACK

with

CHUBBY JOHNSON
MARY ELLEN KAY
MICHAEL CHAPIN
ROY BARCROFT

Directed by
PHILIP FORD
WRITTEN BY
M. COATES WEBST
A REPUBLIC PIC

Some of the Western outlaws—Billy the Kid, Jesse and Frank James and the Younger brothers—become household names. Tales of their crimes and their deeds, often exaggerated, spread throughout the nation. Stories are also told of frontier lawmen like Wyatt Earp and Wild Bill Hickock. As settlements grow and the land becomes populated with law-abiding citizens, the outlaws will be killed or driven from the territory. But these outlaws and lawmen will become part of the growing legend of the West.

I'll sing you a true song of
Billy the Kid;
I'll sing of the desp'rate
deeds that he did.
'Way out in New Mexico
long, long ago,
When a man's only chance
was his old forty-four.

—From song, "Billy the Kid"

THE CHANGING WEST

Though he will become famous, the cowboy's glory days are few in number. While he tends cattle, millions of other Americans are determined to farm the rich prairie soil of the West and to build homes and settlements there. Many of the new settlers raise flocks of sheep for their wool and for the food these animals provide. To keep their sheep contained, they erect fences, which begin to close off the open range. Bitter range wars break out between cattlemen and sheep owners. They are wars that the cattlemen are destined to lose. Every year brings more settlers and a different way of life to the territories where the cowboys once freely roamed.

ens of thousands of early pioneer settlers make the long journey west in covered wagons. By the 1870's, the growing American railroad system brings millions more. The trains can go almost anywhere, as new building methods allow them to cross the widest rivers and pass over the deepest gorges. Now it is no longer necessary for cowboys to drive cattle to far-off railroad towns; the railroad comes to the range. The long cattle drive becomes a thing of the past.

> *We ourselves and the life that we lead will shortly pass away from the plains as completely as the red and white hunters who have vanished from before our herds. . . The broad and boundless prairies have already been bounded and . . . the tide of white settlement during the last few years has risen over the west like a flood and the cattlemen are . . . soon to be overtaken.*
>
> —Theodore Roosevelt, writing on his life as a cowboy, c. 1885

The pioneer farmers are determined and courageous. They will endure many hardships, but they will tame the land and build new lives for themselves and their children. They will see towns and cities rise on the once-empty prairie. In the process, they will continue to fence in the land further cutting off the open range.

By the 1890's the great era of the cowboy is over. In 1886, the cattlemen suffer a bitter blow when an enormous blizzard kills more than 500,000 cattle. But it is the closing of the open range and the end of the long cattle drive that bring the cowboy's life to an end. The land he has traveled upon will never be the same.

I'm going to leave old Texas now,
For they've got no use for the
*   longhorn cow.*
They've plowed and fenced my
*   cattle range,*
And the people there are all so strange.

—From song,
"I'm Going to Leave Old Texas Now"

THE FAMOUS COWBOY

COL.W.F.CODY

But while the cowboy's days on the range may be over, his days as a mythical hero are just beginning. As Americans start to realize that the cattleman is vanishing, a flood of magazines and books bursts upon the scene, describing his way of life, which has been the envy of so many city dwellers for years.

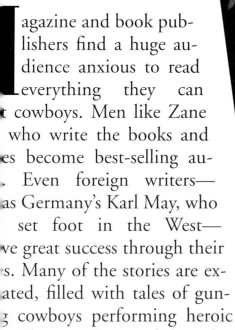

agazine and book publishers find a huge audience anxious to read everything they can cowboys. Men like Zane who write the books and es become best-selling au. Even foreign writers— as Germany's Karl May, who set foot in the West— ve great success through their s. Many of the stories are exated, filled with tales of gung cowboys performing heroic . The popularity of these books and magazines inspires who write and produce stage plays. They create producthat, even more than the magazines and books, exaggerate attleman's life.

In real life, it would have been dangerous
a cowhand to carry a gun while roping ca
or putting down a stampede. But p
wrights quickly discover that their audie
thrill to stories of cowboys ready to fi
weapon in the cause of justice. They also
that plays in which a cowboy captures the h
of a beautiful woman through his heroics
surefire box-office hits.

The cowboy himself adds to the growing fascination. In the early 1900's, showmen bring the rodeo to the cities back east. The rodeo features cowboys competing for prizes by attempting to ride wild bucking horses and fierce bulls. It also features riding, roping and shooting contests. The rodeo adds to the myth of the cowboy as a man who spent most of his time in wild activity.

Wild horses, wild cattle, wild cowboys. What a time we had!

—Visitor to 1874 rodeo

One of the features of every rodeo is the appearance of female contestants. Audiences are amazed at their skill and daring. Some of the cowgirls become even more famous than the men against whom they compete.

FREE STRAWBERRY ROAN RODEO | SEPT. 20
STATE FAIR | OCT. 1
TO

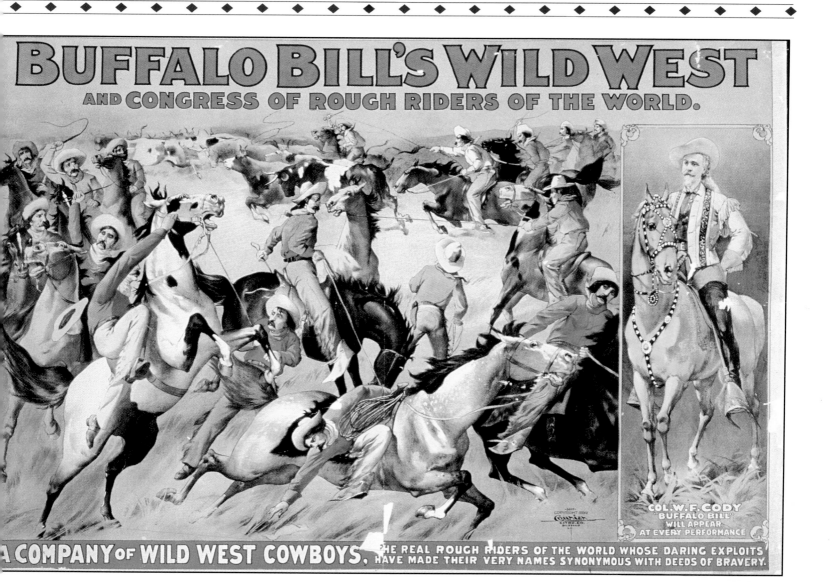

BUFFALO BILL'S WILD WEST
AND CONGRESS OF ROUGH RIDERS OF THE WORLD.

COL. W. F. CODY
"BUFFALO BILL"
WILL APPEAR
AT EVERY PERFORMANCE

A COMPANY OF WILD WEST COWBOYS. THE REAL ROUGH RIDERS OF THE WORLD WHOSE DARING EXPLOITS HAVE MADE THEIR VERY NAMES SYNONYMOUS WITH DEEDS OF BRAVERY.

s exciting as it is, the rodeo pales in comparison to another type of performance that begins to appear in towns and cities throughout America. It is Buffalo Bill's Wild West Show. Buffalo Bill, whose real name is William Cody, is the nation's most famous cowboy. His show includes hundreds of cowboys, cowgirls and Indians. It features plays in which cowboys leap from their horses to halt runaway stage coaches, bank robbers and battle Indians to the death.

BUFFALO BILL'S WILD WEST.
IN THE GRANDEST OF ILLUMINATED ARENAS

LIGHTER THAN DAY

AND CONGRESS OF ROUGH RIDERS OF THE WORLD
2 ELECTRIC PLANTS 250,000 CANDLE POW

2 PERFORMANCES DAILY - "THE RACE OF RACES" THE SHOW OF SHOWS RAIN OR SHINE

Buffalo Bill's Wild West Show becomes an enorm success. It plays to huge audiences not only in Ame but also in Europe. By portraying the cowhand superhero rather than showing the real things he the Wild West Show spreads misconceptions about the c boy around the world.

KEN MAYNARD'S
songs of the trails

SPECIAL ARRANGEMENT
OF SONGS
EACH SONG HAS MELODY,
UKELELE CHORDS, WORDS,
PIANO ACCOMPANIMENT,
AND GUITAR CHORDS

SENSATIONAL SONGS
SUCH AS
HEELS OF DESTINY (THEME SONG)
E TRAIL HERD (THEME SONG)
GIN' ON THE RANGE
AH CARROLL   TRAIL OF MEMORY
AND 20 OTHERS

Published by   M.M.COLE Publishing Co.,   Chicago

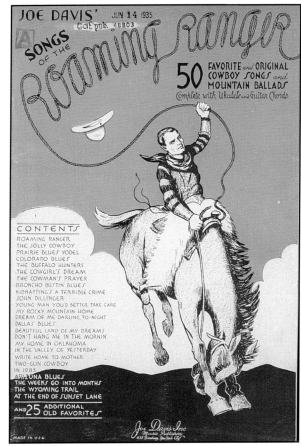

As magazines, books and plays about the cowboy become increasingly popular, so do the many songs that have been written about him over the years. Music stores are filled with cowboy songs. In living rooms and parlors across the nation, Americans listen to these songs on one of their proudest possessions—the newly invented phonograph.

TUMBLING TUMBLEWEEDS

by
BOB NOLAN

featured by
HUM and STRUM
NBC ARTISTS

The cowboy songs add to the grow[ing] legend of the cattleman. They em[pha]size his devotion to duty, his lov[e of] nature and his lonesome way of lif[e.]

PATENT LEATHER BOOT[S]

A JOHN KLENNER
BOB MILLER SONG

BOB MILLER
MUSIC · PUBLISHER
1619 BROADWAY   NEW YOR[K]

here is an even greater invention than the phonograph. As a new century begins, the motion picture is perfected. Americans by the millions in a love affair with the movies, and it through the movies that the cowboy's e as a mythical hero is most firmly lished.

THE SHERIFF'S REWARD
HEART TAKEN PRISONER
COWBOY DRAMA

Selig

TRADE S MARK

"THE CATTLE THIEVES ARE AFTER YOU!"

ADOLPH ZUKOR presents

ZANE GREY'S

Wagon Wheels

WITH RANDOLPH SCOTT, GAIL PATRICK
MONTE BLUE, RAYMOND HATTON
BILLY LEE   A PARAMOUNT PICTURE

JOHNNY MACK BROWN

in

OKLAHOMA FRONTIER

with **BOB BAKER**
Fuzzy KNIGHT

ANNE GWYNNE

and *Famed Cowboy Troubadours of Radio*
THE TEXAS RANGERS

> *The hero of all these movies is a cowboy without cattle.*
> —Movie critic, c. 1920

n the movies, and ater on television, cowboys become the washbucklers of the t. There are "good " and "bad guys." re are constant gun- ts, stagecoach hold- and battles with ans, outlaws and r cowboys. All that made the maga- s, books and stage s so successful is hasized to an even ter degree by the iemakers. Because the popularity of ern songs, they create a new type hero—the singing boy.

y the end of the first decade of the 1900's, the cowboy has become larger than life. His picture is everywhere, particularly in packaging and advertising.

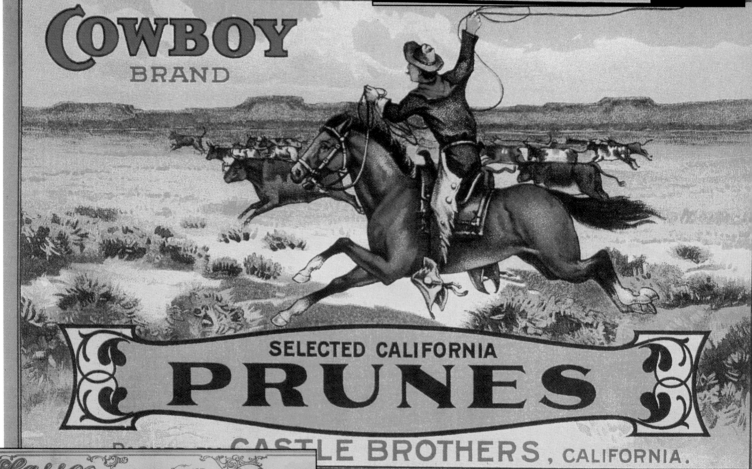

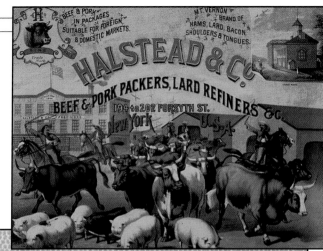

ike the authors, stage and movie producers and song publishers, advertisers know that the cowboy is a hero who appeals to all Americans. They fill their ads with his picture. They create products that inspire even the most hardened dwellers to dress like cowboys.

"TESTING"
CLARK'S O.N.T. SPOOL COTTON.

THE COWBOY TODAY

Through songs and stories, books and films, the American cowboy grows into our most famous legendary figure. The cowboy's way of life does not vanish completely; there are still men and women who carry on the traditions set by cowhands more than one hundred years ago.

Throughout the West there are modern cowboys who spend their days in the saddle. They have modern advantages that the original cowpunchers could never have imagined. Helicopter pilots circling the range let today's cowhands know by [radio] where they can find wandering cattle. Jeeps deliver hot [lunc]hes from the ranch house to wherever the cowboys are working. [But] as in the old days, the cowboys' main object of attention is still [c]attle.

The herding and breeding of cattle . . . is . . . the grand, independent, health-giving, out-of-doors existence, the praises of which have been sung through all the ages. To how many a pale, thin, hard-working city dweller does the thought of "the cattle on a thousand hills" . . . and the sight of the mighty mountains bring strangely vivid emotions and longings.

—Harper's Magazine, c. 1880

While it is on a far smaller scale, the work remains the same. Horses still have to be broken and trained to separate calves from the herd. The riding and roping skills developed by the earlier cowhands are just as important to today's cowboys.

ust as in days gone by, the roundup is still one of the most important events in the cowboy's year. The final activity of the roundup
remains the branding of the cattle, a process carried out almost
exactly as it was over one hundred years ago.

There is still the cattle drive, too. The drives are much shorter now. The animals are shipped to ma[rket] from places close to where they are raised. But they still need to be driven from summer range to [win]ter pasture. The most experienced cowhands still ride the point, other cowhands protect the fl[anks,] and the dust kicked up by the herd still covers the faces of those who ride at the rear.

The cowboy's glory days are over. But as long as there are men and women [who] prefer to work in [open] air and open sky, as [long] as there are those [who] are as comfortable [on] horseback as they are [on] the ground, as long as [the]re are cattle to tend, [the]re will be cowboys.

The American cowboy is emblazoned in our memory. We cannot forget him. He still affects much of the way we dress, the songs we sing, the way we talk and the way we think.

THE LOG OF A COWBOY

BY ANDY ADAMS

He is perhaps the most American of us all. His restlessness, his optimism, his joy in hard work, his love of adventure, his spirit of independence, are the very qualities that mark us as a nation.

is place as one of our greatest heroes is secure. Much of it is due to the myths that surround him, but much more is due to what he really did and who he really was. Perhaps our greatest fascination with him comes from the fact that, more than we realize, there is a little bit of the cowboy in us all.

The Library of Congress

ll of the photographs, lithographs, engravings, paintings, line drawings, posters, song lyrics, song-sheet covers, broadsides and other illustrative materials contained in this book have been culled from the collections of the Library of Congress. The Library houses the largest collection of stored knowledge on earth. Within its walls lie treasures that show us how much more than a "library" a great library can be.

he statistics that help define the Library are truly amazing. It has more books from America and England
 anywhere else, yet barely one half of its collections are in English. It contains more maps, globes, charts
 atlases than any other place on earth. It houses one of the largest collections of photographs in the world,
 largest collection of films in America, almost every phonograph record ever made in the United States
 the collections of the American Folklife Center. The Library also contains over six million volumes on
 sciences and applied technology.

is a very modern institution as well. Dr. James Billington, the Librarian of Congress, has defined the Li-
y's future through his vision of a "library without walls." "I see the Library of Congress in the future," he
said, "as an active catalyst for civilization, not just a passive mausoleum of cultural accomplishments of
past." A good example of this commitment is the Library's National Demonstration Laboratory, which,
ugh hands-on work stations, offers over 200 examples of the latest innovations in interactive video and
puter learning.

he Library of Congress was originally established to serve the members of Congress. Over the years it has
ved into a great national library. Unlike almost every other national library in the world, the Library of
gress does not limit the use of its collections to accredited scholars. Ours is a national library made by the
ple for the people, and is open to all the people. Fondly referred to as "the storehouse of the national
nory," it is truly one of our proudest and most important possessions.

Index

Numbers in *italics* indicate photographs, maps, and illustrations.